Mathematics and Computing/Technology
An Inter-faculty Second Level Course

MT262 Putting Computer Systems to Work

# Block III
Developing Visual Programs

# Unit 2
Designing Interfaces

Prepared for the Course Team by Bob Margolis

This text forms part of the Open University second-level course MT262 *Putting Computer Systems to Work*, which among other things teaches the use of Borland C$^{++}$Builder 5 Standard to tackle small programming projects. (Borland C$^{++}$Builder 5 Standard is copyright © 2000 Borland International (UK) Limited.)

The course software comprises the Borland C$^{++}$Builder 5 Standard CD-ROM and the MT262 Templates and Libraries CD-ROM, both of which are supplied as part of the course.

This publication forms part of an Open University course. Details of this and other Open University courses can be obtained from the Course Information and Advice Centre, PO Box 724, The Open University, Milton Keynes, MK7 6ZS, United Kingdom: tel. +44 (0)1908 653231, e-mail general-enquiries@open.ac.uk

Alternatively, you may visit the Open University website at http://www.open.ac.uk where you can learn more about the wide range of courses and packs offered at all levels by The Open University.

To purchase a selection of Open University course materials, visit the webshop at www.ouw.co.uk, or contact Open University Worldwide, Michael Young Building, Walton Hall, Milton Keynes, MK7 6AA, United Kingdom, for a brochure: tel. +44 (0)1908 858785, fax +44 (0)1908 858787, e-mail ouwenq@open.ac.uk

The Open University, Walton Hall, Milton Keynes, MK7 6AA.

First published 1999. Second edition 2002.

Copyright © 2002 The Open University

All rights reserved; no part of this publication may be reproduced, stored in a retrieval system, transmitted or utilised in any form or by any means, electronic, mechanical, photocopying, recording or otherwise, without written permission from the publisher or a licence from the Copyright Licensing Agency Ltd. Details of such licences (for reprographic reproduction) may be obtained from the Copyright Licensing Agency Ltd, 90 Tottenham Court Road, London W1T 4LP.

Open University course materials may also be made available in electronic formats for use by students of the University. All rights, including copyright and related rights and database rights, in electronic course materials and their contents are owned by or licensed to The Open University, or otherwise used by The Open University as permitted by applicable law.

In using electronic course materials and their contents you agree that your use will be solely for the purposes of following an Open University course of study or otherwise as licensed by The Open University or its assigns.

Except as permitted above you undertake not to copy, store in any medium (including electronic storage or use in a website), distribute, transmit or re-transmit, broadcast, modify or show in public such electronic materials in whole or in part without the prior written consent of The Open University or in accordance with the Copyright, Designs and Patents Act 1988.

Edited, designed and typeset by The Open University, using the Open University T$_{E}$X System.

Printed in the United Kingdom by Martins the Printers, Berwick-upon-Tweed

ISBN 0 7492 4096 2

2.2

# Contents

| | | |
|---|---|---|
| Introduction | | 5 |
| 1 | A visual warehouse design | 8 |
| 2 | Components for the design | 16 |
| | 2.1 Selecting components | 16 |
| | 2.2 Creating menus | 18 |
| 3 | Coding the design | 21 |
| 4 | Inheritance and wrapping | 29 |
| 5 | Multi-window designs | 32 |
| Objectives | | 40 |
| Appendix: Conventions | | 41 |
| Solutions to the Exercises | | 42 |
| Solutions to the Computer Activities | | 48 |
| Index | | 53 |

# Study guide

A recommended study pattern, based on an average overall study time, is as follows.

| Material | Study time |
| --- | --- |
| Introduction, Section 1 (text) | 1 hour |
| Section 2 (computer) | $1\frac{1}{2}$ hours |
| Section 3 (computer) | $3\frac{1}{2}$ hours |
| Section 4 (text) | 1 hour |
| Section 5 (computer) | $3\frac{1}{2}$ hours |

You will need access to your computer whilst studying Sections 2, 3 and 5.

Section 4 is a reading section, which sets Sections 1 to 3 in context.

In addition to the five sections, there is an appendix. The first item in the appendix lists some 'ground rules' concerning *Windows* programs that are adopted in MT262. The second concerns naming conventions for certain values of the properties of some components in the Builder toolkit. Both items will be useful points of reference.

A note on terminology is appropriate here. Strictly speaking, a declaration such as

`int AnInteger;`

declares an **instance**, called *AnInteger* of the data type **int**. For brevity, *AnInteger* has been referred to as an integer variable, or just an integer. It is normal to take a little more care with terminology when working with an object-based toolkit. You will be making much use of the class library that forms the basis of the Builder toolkit. The class library defines a collection of classes, that is, object data types. Your programs will contain objects which are instances of classes. The course will refer to the types as classes (as before) and will reserve the term 'object' for an instance (variable) of a class type. Thus, for example, *TButton* is the Builder class representing a *Windows* button; a particular button (that is, instance of the class *TButton*) would be referred to as an object.

This unit makes a number of course team versions of Builder projects available. These projects are complete, so that you may compile and run them in order to compare and check your coding of the designs against those of the course team.

All the C++ *coding* in the course team project files will be the same as yours is intended to be (apart from one or two intentional exceptions). What will be different are some of the `#include` lines that Builder inserts automatically, as well as some of the manually inserted lines. The reason is that course team file names are different from yours, being prefixed by `CT`. The course team felt that the advantage to you of being able to *run* the course team projects outweighed the disadvantage of having to cope with these slight differences.

# Introduction

The unit will extend the design ideas that were started in *Unit 1*, and will also explore further the facilities offered by Builder's Visual Component Library. As with the earlier work, it is important to bear in mind that although the details are *Windows*-specific, the general principles apply to other *Windows*-like operating systems.

It is important to make clear that a very restricted view is taken here of 'designing' a visual interface. As mentioned in *Unit 1* of Block I, there are complex and important issues connected with the principles of interface design. In this course, the course team take, for good or ill, the conventions that have developed over the years for *Windows* programs. (Examples include placing any `File` menu on the far left of the main menu, as in Builder and *Windows* word-processing programs for example, and underlining the `F` in `File` to indicate the keyboard shortcut.) Although not all features of interfaces are covered by these conventions, a number are. You will meet a number of these conventions in this unit. A list of 'ground rules' adopted in MT262 is given in the Appendix.

Adopting these conventions may not lead to the interface that would be 'best' in some absolute sense, but should enable users to cope with your programs without too much reading of any program manual you might provide.

An underlying theme of this unit is how to adapt classes provided by a library to the task in hand. One of the strengths of object-oriented programming (and languages like C$^{++}$ that support objects) is that ways of adapting objects are available. In particular, in this unit, you will see the use of **inheritance** and **wrapping**, which are applicable to all C$^{++}$ compilers. You will also see some techniques that apply only to the extensions to C$^{++}$ which Builder provides specifically for *Windows* programming. The properties and event handlers which you used in *Unit 1* are *not* part of the C$^{++}$ language, they are *Windows*-specific extensions.

One of the things that you may already have noticed is that loops apparently play a relatively small part in designs for visual programs. A typical console application has a top-level design which is some variation on the following.

1     initialise as necessary
2     **loop while** there is still data to be processed
3         process data
4     **loopend**
5     present results if necessary

Asking for input and presenting results may also be done within the loop. Your work with *Windows* programs in *Unit 1* does not seem to fit this basic pattern. However, this top-level design *is* still present, but well hidden. It is hidden partly in the way that the operating system and a program interact, and partly in the code that Builder provides for you.

The top-level design for a *Windows* program is, effectively,

1   initialise as necessary
2   **loop**
3       **if** an event has occurred for this program **then**
4           handle the event
5       **ifend**
6   **loopend when** user closes program

Step 4, handling the event, refines to a large multi-way **switch** statement to deal with any of the (literally) hundreds of different events that the operating system can send to the program. Fortunately, the code generated automatically by Builder handles the vast majority of these events with sensible default behaviour, so that you have to handle only the events that are specific to your program.

Thus, an overall loop structure is still there, but you do not have to design and code it for each program. Nor do you have to deal with routine tasks, some of which can be substantial. For example, if your program window is, temporarily, covered by another that the user is working with, then when your program window is revealed again, its contents must be redrawn on the screen. The classes that you will make use of know how to redraw themselves, so you do not have to know how to draw them.

This discussion should help to explain the central role played by event handlers in *Windows* programming. By writing event handlers, you adapt the behaviour of objects (instances, or variables, of particular class types) so that they do what the problem demands. For example, a button has various sorts of behaviour built in, including how to appear 'pressed down' when the mouse pointer is clicked over it. You adapt a button for a specific purpose by adding an event handler to carry out other processing when the button is clicked.

In this unit you will be using a variety of classes from the Visual Component Library, which is part of the Builder toolkit. As you know from *Unit 1*, Borland refer to classes that represent visual devices as **components**. (For example, in *Unit 1* you used the components *Button* and *Panel*.)

There are some non-visual components as well.

The course team suggest that, if time permits, you look at the Help system entry for any class that you are asked to use. (The activities that you will be asked to do will use only a small proportion of the capabilities of some of the classes.) Consulting the Help system will assist you in building up a picture of what is available to help you design and code solutions to your own problems.

To make things easier for you, Borland use a consistent naming convention in their visual component class library: class names always begin with '*T*'. For example, buttons are instances (variables) of type *TButton*. As you know from *Unit 1*, to find out all about the *TButton* class, you select `Help|C++Builder Help|Index` and type *TButton* into the box on the Index page. Clicking on `Display` will bring up the reference page, with links to lists of the properties, methods and events associated with buttons.

This convention is a hangover from the days when Borland language compilers were always 'Turbo-something' because of their pride in the speed of compiling. You might like to think of it as standing for 'type'.

As well as making you more familiar with the use of a class library and adapting classes, this unit is intended to develop further your systematic

approach to designing solutions. Having decided a top-level design for a solution, the following aspects will usually appear in some order.
- Designing the visual appearance of the program, based on the top-level design.
- Deciding the behaviours wanted from each button, menu option, etc.
- Designing the processing to be done in each event handler.
- Designing the engine, if needed.

As you have seen in *Unit 1*, the second and third steps above are usually dealt with in two stages, corresponding respectively to the visual effects and non-visual effects required of each event handler. It is often helpful to adopt the 'interface plus engine' approach used in *Unit 1* to separate the visual and non-visual processing into different modules. If this is appropriate, then the event handlers usually deal with visual matters directly, and then call methods of one (or more) objects in the 'engine' module to do the rest of the processing.

This description of the design process skates over a considerable difficulty. When building a program using a large toolkit, such as Builder's, there is the problem of tracking down something in the toolkit that either does what you want or can be adapted to do it. For some things, menus and buttons for example, finding out what the toolkit offers is not too hard. For, say, displaying results of a calculation and entering data, it may be harder to find out whether something suitable is available and, if so, what it is called. In such cases, you will be guided appropriately.

The coding follows much the same division as the design process.
- Designing the visual appearance of the program by dropping the appropriate components onto forms. This *is* coding, although the actual code is written by Builder.
- Modifying the properties of components so that they have appropriate captions, colours, etc.
- Coding the designs for the event handlers.
- Coding the engine, if used.

The process of compiling and running the code should, normally, be done regularly during the coding. The visual appearance can be checked quite early on, even though none of the components will *do* anything. A systematic approach should be taken to coding the event handlers. All the visual actions can be coded, followed by all the non-visual ones, or both aspects of each event handler can be completed in turn. Usually, it is helpful to complete the visual actions first. The reason is that these actions normally include making sure that only appropriate user input is possible at each stage. Thus, for the Mean problem in *Unit 1*, the Done button was disabled until at least one number had been processed, so that calculating the mean could not take place until calculating a mean made sense. As each event handler has code added, the program should be run to check for bugs.

It is quite usual for *Windows* programs to use more than one window. For example, Builder can have a number of windows open when running: the Code Editor, the Object Inspector, the Watch List, and so on. There is actually a transparent window as well, to which all these belong, which is why they all disappear together when you minimise Builder.

Section 1 revisits the Warehouse problem from Block II. Designing a *Windows* interface for this will illustrate a lot of the points about design. One thing that should become apparent is that the design process is inherently modular. Once a visual design has been decided, the actions to

> In *Unit 1*, you located the icon for the *MainMenu* component, but you did not use it. In this unit, you will make much use of this component.

be taken when a menu option (or button, or ...) is selected *must* be considered separately because the user can select any of them in any order.

Section 2 discusses the problem of selecting components to implement a design, and introduces you to the use of the *MainMenu* component. It also introduces some ideas that arise from the initial design such as the grouping of components.

In Section 3, you are asked to complete the practical coding of the design based on Sections 1 and 2. This involves a great deal of practical work with Builder but each part of the code can be tested as it is written, so bug-finding should not be too difficult.

Section 4 reviews the first three sections and discusses some of the underlying ideas that are revealed by the code that Builder has generated for the warehouse project.

Finally, Section 5 considers a rather different approach to designing the warehouse interface. In the procedural version of Block II, the user had to complete an activity such as a delivery before starting to process an order. The visual interface developed in Sections 1 to 3 follows this approach. In the *Windows* environment, it is possible to have several windows open at once. The user could work on a delivery, switch to another window to process an urgent order, then continue with the delivery. The design of such interfaces is considered in Section 5; it introduces some new ideas about *Windows* programming.

# 1 A visual warehouse design

In this section you are asked to tackle the problem of designing a *Windows* interface for the Warehouse problem of Block II. You are provided with a slightly modified version of the file containing the *WarehouseType* and *BinType* classes, and the problem is to design a suitable 'user interface' to this code. In many ways, this is a common type of problem: a new interface to existing processing code is required. If the interaction with the user in such a problem is too bound up with the processing, then the task is sometimes hopeless. But if the original design is properly modular, as is the case here, then the task may well be possible. The way the problem arises means that an 'interface plus engine' approach is actually forced on us; also, the engine module (the warehouse representation) already exists.

To be quite specific, a problem specification follows.

## Problem Specification  Visual Warehouse

Design and code a *Windows* interface to the warehouse class. The methods available in that class, each with a comment outlining its purpose, are listed below. (They are taken from the header file B3WHImpl.h.)

```
void Init(AnsiString Filename);
  // Initialises warehouse using data stored in Filename if that
  // file exists; otherwise, initialises warehouse to be empty

void Save(AnsiString Filename);
  // Saves current state of warehouse in file called Filename,
  // overwriting existing file of that name (if any)

AnsiString Store(int InCode, int InQuantity);
  // Stores quantity InQuantity of product with code InCode if possible
  // String returned says where to place product or is an error message
  // Updates warehouse internal information

AnsiString Supply(int OutCode, int OutQuantity);
  // Supplies quantity OutQuantity of product with code OutCode
  // returning information about location(s) or an error message
  // Updates warehouse internal information
```

To make this class available to the interface that you will design in Section 3, the header file B3WHImpl.h should be #included and the library file B3WHImpl.lib added to the Builder project. You will also need to declare an instance of the *WarehouseType* class. But you will *not* have to consider the design and coding of the *WarehouseType* class and its methods. These tasks have been done and the class is available for use.

The interface design should allow the user to choose to process a delivery to the warehouse, process an order, or quit. The user must also be able to indicate that a particular delivery or order (probably consisting of a number of items) has been completed. The interface should allow the state of the warehouse to be read from a file and saved to a file as necessary. Within the limits of what the interface is to do, it should look as much like a standard *Windows* program as possible, that is it should make use of menus, buttons, etc., as appropriate.  □

This problem specification is fairly general and there are several very loosely specified items, particularly those connected with reading and saving the state of the warehouse.

Given the ease with which visual components can be added, it seems reasonable to begin with a simple design.

A standard *Windows* program almost always has a main menu from which the user can choose the action to be performed. Convention demands that, if any files are involved, the `File` menu occupies the leftmost position on the main menu. By convention, the `Exit` or `Quit` option always appears on the **drop-down menu** list for the `File` menu, if there is such a menu. There *is* a file associated with this problem: the one containing the state of the warehouse. Thus, a `File` menu is required and should probably have `Open` and `Save` options, as well as `Exit`. (Whilst `Load` might seem a more natural name for the menu option which loads the warehouse contents from a file, convention dictates the use of `Open`.)

*Exit will be used rather than Quit.*

This interface will require another menu concerned with deliveries and orders. Using the same term as in the original problem, the course team settled on `Activity` for this, with two options `Delivery` and `Order`. The sketch below illustrates the menu as envisaged. But note that while this sketch shows both the drop-down menu lists, one under `File` and one under `Activity`, in practice, only one of these menus can be visible at one time.

*The line between `Save` and `Exit` will be discussed in Section 2.*

| File | Activity |
|------|----------|
| Open | Delivery |
| Save | Order    |
| Exit |          |

Working with menus should be familiar to you. For present purposes you should think of the menu options as having much behaviour in common with buttons. Menu options can be selected — provided they are visible and enabled — and selection triggers their *OnClick* event, for which appropriate code will have to be written.

### Exercise 1.1

Indicate, in broad terms, what each menu option in the above figure should do.

[*Solution on page 42*]

The visual interface must involve much more than the main menu and the drop-down menus. For example, to cope with a delivery the interface has to provide a means by which the user can enter data for the various codes and quantities making up the delivery. In the rest of this subsection you are asked to develop, and complete, the visual design.

### Exercise 1.2

What additional things are required in the interface to deal with deliveries and orders?

[*Solution on page 42*]

The discussion so far suggests a visual design of the form shown in the following figure. Two edit boxes are represented, with labels, in the data entry area. The results area must be able to display several lines of text. The drop-down menus for `File` and `Activity` are not shown here.

You met the edit box and label components in *Unit 1*.

It is at this point that it is possible to make use of the *Windows* environment in a way that was not possible in the 'console application' version. In that version, a code or quantity value was accepted on pressing the `Enter` key. It is now possible to allow the user to key in both values, and to provide a button to indicate that the user is happy with the entries. Thus, a button with caption `Accept` could be added. Equally, rather than using a sentinel value (code of zero) to indicate that the delivery (or order) is finished, a button with caption `Finished` can be provided for that purpose. The following figure summarises this thinking on the design.

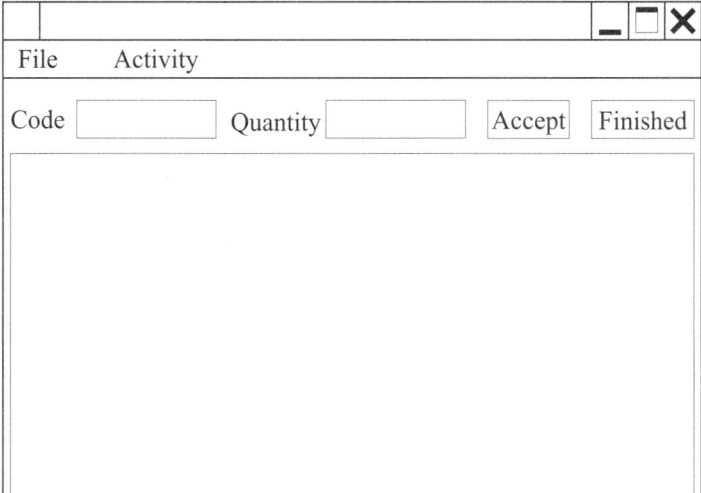

Now that a basic visual design exists, the initial settings and the event handlers have to be considered. An event will be generated by the operating system whenever the user chooses a menu option or presses a button, so the response to each action by the user has to be designed. The approach that is adopted here is to consider the visual effects of each event in detail, but only sketching in the actual data processing.

11

### Exercise 1.3

Suggest initial states for the various menu options, boxes and buttons with which the user can interact.

[*Solution on page 42*]

---

The visual effects of the event handlers at run-time are now considered in turn. None of the `File` menu options affect the properties of other visual components (except that selection of the `Exit` option causes the program to close). When the `Delivery` option from the `Activity` menu is chosen, the following should happen.

- The data entry area should be prepared for the user inputs. This involves ensuring that the two buttons and two edit boxes are enabled, and the edit boxes are cleared of text. In addition, focus should be given to the Code edit box.
- Something in the window has to inform the user that it is a delivery now being processed, and not an order. The window title bar — the form's Caption — can be used for this purpose.

*The `File` menu options will be considered at the end of the section.*

### Exercise 1.4

What visual effects do you anticipate occurring when the user chooses `Activity|Order`.

[*Solution on page 42*]

---

If a delivery or order is being processed, clicking the `Accept` button will provoke some processing. The values in the two edit boxes will be read and sent to the warehouse engine for processing. As a result of this, some output will appear in the display area. (You will be able to spell out what this output will be when the processing has been considered.) In preparation for the next entry, the data in the edit boxes should be cleared, and focus should be returned to the Code box.

### Exercise 1.5

If a delivery or order is being processed, what should the visual effect(s) of pressing the `Finished` button be?

[*Solution on page 43*]

---

There are other sensible decisions that can be taken at this stage, to control the user's handling of the program. As only one activity is to be taking place at one time, the `Finished` button and the `Activity` menu can be paired in the following sense. When an activity is selected, the `Activity` menu is disabled until this activity — a delivery or an order — is finished. The finish is indicated by clicking the `Finished` button. Adapting this approach, the `Finished` button should enable the `Activity` menu and disable the edit boxes and buttons in the data entry area.

*In Section 5 several activities are allowed to happen simultaneously. Different decisions will be needed here for that situation.*

The discussion of the `Activity|Delivery` menu option event handler leads to the following top-level design.

Activity|Delivery

1. prepare data entry area
2. disable `Activity` menu
3. set form's caption to indicate "Delivery"

The top-level design for the `Activity|Order` menu option event handler is almost identical to that for `Activity|Delivery`. The only difference is that the final step must reflect that the current activity is an order.

Activity|Order

1. prepare data entry area
2. disable `Activity` menu
3. set form's caption to indicate "Order"

The event handler for the `Accept` button is where the real work of interacting with the engine — the warehouse object — has to be done. This is where a slight problem arises: there is a single button, but it has to have slightly different effects depending on whether a delivery or an order is currently being processed. For a delivery, the warehouse object is to be asked to store an item; for an order, it must supply an item. Since there are only two possibilities, a boolean variable can be used to indicate which type of activity is currently being processed. Thus, the variable would have value **true** if a delivery is being processed, and **false** if an order is being processed. The value of this variable at the time of clicking the `Accept` button will determine which message to send to the engine.

*This choice is arbitrary: the values could equally well be the other way round.*

Now, a data table for the Visual Warehouse problem can be considered. Integer variables for the product code and quantity will be needed. A boolean variable to control the behaviour of the `Accept` button is also needed, as discussed above.

*The variables created by Builder when constructing the form are not included in this data table.*

| Type | Identifier | Description |
| --- | --- | --- |
| Integer | *Code* | Product code of item being processed |
| Integer | *Quantity* | Product quantity of item being processed |
| Boolean | *IsDelivery* | **true** for a delivery, **false** for an order |

It is now possible to add to the top-level design for the `Activity|Delivery` menu option event handler to take account of the need to set *IsDelivery* to the correct value.

Activity|Delivery

1. prepare data entry area
2. disable `Activity` menu
3. set form's caption to indicate "Delivery"
4. *IsDelivery* ← **true**

### Exercise 1.6

Write down the extra step needed by the top-level design for the `Activity|Order` menu option event handler to bring it to the stage equivalent to that which the `Activity|Delivery` event handler has reached.

[*Solution on page 43*]

---

It is now possible to consider the processing caused by `Accept` button being clicked. From earlier discussion, the action will depend on the value of *IsDelivery*, which implies an **if... then...** structure for the design. If *IsDelivery* is true, then the *Store* method of the warehouse object needs to be used; if it is not true, the *Supply* method will be the correct method. The complicating factor concerns reading the data. The entries made by the user in the boxes are strings, but both the warehouse methods mentioned require integers as inputs. There has to be a conversion process, which may fail if the user has typed in something that does not represent a valid integer. Fortunately, as you will see in Section 3, the string to integer conversion facilities of C++ allow a default value to be specified in case conversion fails. Because zero is not a valid product code or quantity, it makes a good default value: the design can attempt both conversions (of code and quantity) and if either results in a zero, then the input can be ignored.

Remembering that the data must be read *before* the edit boxes are cleared, a design (for the event handler for the `Accept` button) resulting from this discussion is as follows.

#### Accept

1   set *Code* to value obtained by converting string to integer (or 0 on failure)
2   set *Quantity* to value obtained by converting string to integer (or 0 on failure)
3   **if** *Code* $> 0$ **and** *Quantity* $> 0$ **then**
4       do necessary processing and write results in display area
5   **ifend**
6   clear *Code* edit box
7   clear *Quantity* edit box
8   give focus to *Code* edit box

The processing in step 4 will depend on the value of *IsDelivery*, so a refinement of that step looks like this.

4.1   **if** *IsDelivery* = *true* **then**
4.2       display *Store*(*Code*, *Quantity*)
4.3   **else**
4.4       ...
4.5   **ifend**

### Exercise 1.7

Write down the missing step 4.4.

## Exercise 1.8

Bearing in mind the solution to Exercise 1.5, write down a top-level design for the event handler when the Finished button is clicked.

[Solutions on page 43]

---

The Activity menu options and the associated buttons have now had their actions designed. The remaining options are the File|Open, File|Save and File|Exit menu options. At first sight, the design for the last of these is the simplest: it should close the program. (Below you are asked to think about other activities that should happen when the program is closed.)

The File|Open and File|Save options will use the *Init* and *Save* methods provided by the warehouse object. In a more elaborate design, the user might be permitted to choose the data file to be used. For now, a fixed file called B3WHData.dat will be used.

## Exercise 1.9

Give suitable (very simple) designs for the event handlers for the File|Open and File|Save options.

## Exercise 1.10

What else might the File|Exit menu option event handler do as well as simply closing the program? (Do not spend too long on this.)

[Solutions on page 43]

---

This concludes a first attempt at the design of a visual interface for the warehouse, together with designs for the actions that various visual components should perform. In the next section, a step towards coding is taken by discussing the selection of suitable components from the Builder toolkit.

# 2 Components for the design

You need to have Builder running for this section although you will be doing very little actual coding.

## 2.1 Selecting components

Having arrived at a design for the warehouse interface, the next question is: what does the Builder toolkit provide so that as little coding as possible is done by hand? The visual design requires the following components (apart from the usual main window):

- a main menu (to house `File` and `Activity`),
- a panel to group the components of the data entry area,
- edit boxes (to type in data),
- buttons,
- labels (for the edit boxes),
- an area in which to display strings (for the results).

*In Unit 1, you were introduced to several components that will be useful for the design of Section 1. However, some additional components will be needed; you will be guided in discovering them.*

In the course of your work exploring Builder's Component Palette, you have located and used components corresponding to all these elements of the design, except the first one. The class for this item is *TMainMenu*; its use will be discussed in the next subsection.

*If you were to look up the Help system entry for the TMainMenu class, you would see that 'TMainMenu encapsulates a menu bar and its accompanying drop-down menus for a form'.*

You have already used the *TPanel* class in *Unit 1*, to group the entry and edit keys and to group the operator keys in the project `CTCalc`. The *Enabled* property of this class will be particularly useful here. (Builder's *Panel* component has many properties and methods that are not present in the equivalent component in other programming environments. It is for this reason that the design in Section 1 did not use the term panel; the more general phrase 'data entry area' was used.)

You have also already met the *TMemo* class for displaying text. An object of this class would be entirely suitable for displaying the (string) information returned by the warehouse's *Supply* and *Store* methods. However, it is quite useful to be aware how the Builder Help system can, with a little persistence on your part, indicate which components might be useful for this task. If you were to select `Help|C++Builder Help|Index`, enter 'text' in the edit box at the top and then select `Display`, you would be offered a list of entries related to 'text'. Pursuing these entries would (eventually!) convince you that there are two components that are intended for working with multiple lines of text: the *TMemo* class, which you have already met, and the *TRichEdit* class.

**Exercise 2.1**

(a) Inspect the descriptions in the Help system entries for the *TMemo* and *TRichEdit* classes.

(b) One of these classes has a *Print* method. Find which class has it. Might the possession of this method help in making a choice between the two classes?

*Use the alphabetical listing of methods to locate the required class.*

[*Solution on page 44*]

Thus, the Builder components that are likely to be useful for implementing the design from Section 1 are as follows.
- a main menu (of type *TMainMenu*),
- a panel (*TPanel*),
- two edit boxes (*TEdit*),
- two buttons (*TButton*),
- two labels (*TLabel*),
- a memo (*TMemo* or *TRichEdit*).

Although the solution to Exercise 2.1 suggested that a *TRichEdit* component might be the better choice if printing is to be involved, the *TMemo* class is somewhat simpler to work with and will be the choice here.

To conclude this subsection, you are asked to complete a data table which includes the components that you will place on the form, and also to investigate the properties and methods that are likely to be used for the coding.

### Exercise 2.2

Complete the following data table so that it includes all components discussed so far.

| Type | Identifier | Description |
|---|---|---|
| *TMainMenu* | *MainMenu* | Main menu for the program window |
| *TLabel* | *CodeLabel* | Label for product code box |
| ... | ... | Label for product quantity box |
| *TEdit* | *CodeBox* | Input box for product code |
| ... | ... | Input box for product quantity |
| *TButton* | *AcceptButton* | Press to accept data in boxes |
| ... | ... | Press to stop processing |
| *TMemo* | ... | Displays information from warehouse object |
| *TPanel* | ... | Groups data entry area items |

As in *Unit 1*, identifiers are chosen to be as descriptive as possible. For example, *CodeLabel* identifies a label component with caption "Code". The Course Team uses the appendix "box" for both *TEdit* and *TMemo* objects; both appear as boxes holding text. For the sake of the readability of your code, it is strongly suggested that you adopt this style.

### Exercise 2.3

In *Unit 1*, you met some of the properties and methods of the five classes *TPanel, TButton, TLabel, TEdit* and *TMemo*. Properties included *Caption, Name, Enabled, Text, ReadOnly* and *Lines*; methods included *Clear* and *SetFocus*. Consider each of the five classes in turn and, by using the Help system as necessary, decide which of the above properties and methods are likely to be useful in coding the designs.

The lists of properties and methods vary from class to class.

For *TMemo*, try to discover a method which will enable a line of text to be added to what is already displayed. (Do not spend too long on this.)

[*Solutions on page 44*]

You will need the solutions to Exercise 2.2 and Exercise 2.3 when you use the form designer to produce the program window in Builder. The identifier column of the data table will give you a check-list for setting the *Name* properties of the components as you add them to the form. You can also use the data table to check that you have set the *Caption* properties correctly (since if a component has a caption, it will 'match' the identifier — *Code* and *CodeLabel*, for example).

The experience of locating the *Add* method, for adding more to a memo, typifies the common difficulty of finding just what a toolkit has to offer. Even when you have found a class that appears to be suitable for implementing a particular design, you may find that it does not have — or you cannot locate — a method to carry out a specific task required. (Some classes, such as *TMemo*, have many methods to search through.) You will be provided with guidance in your searching. As your experience grows, you will become familiar with what methods and properties to look for.

## 2.2 Creating menus

In Section 3 you are going to code the visual interface design from Section 1 for the Warehouse problem of Block II. To that end you are going to be making much use of the component *MainMenu*. The following experiments are intended to introduce you to the uses of menus having a drop-down list of options. As in the previous unit, the bulleted activities are short, and there are no formal solutions: the text following each such activity provides relevant comment.

You should have Builder running with `Block III` as the current folder.

○ Open a new application and save it as `Expt6` in the `Block III` folder. Select *MainMenu* from the Component Palette, and drop a menu onto the form (anywhere). Double-click on the menu icon on the form.

If you have forgotten how to do this, consult *Unit 1* or the Handbook.

The **menu editor** should have opened, with title `Form1->MainMenu1`. This is where you create a main menu to go with a form. Creating the menu itself is very straightforward; the real work comes when the processing to implement selection of a particular menu option has to be written.

○ The menu editor is poised ready for entry of the first menu. First make sure the Object Inspector is open. Now type "Colour", but do not press `Enter` yet. (Note that "Colour" has been entered in the Object Inspector as the *Caption* property.) Now press `Enter`. This creates a Colour menu, and the editor prepares for entry of the first option in this menu's drop-down list, as shown below (left).

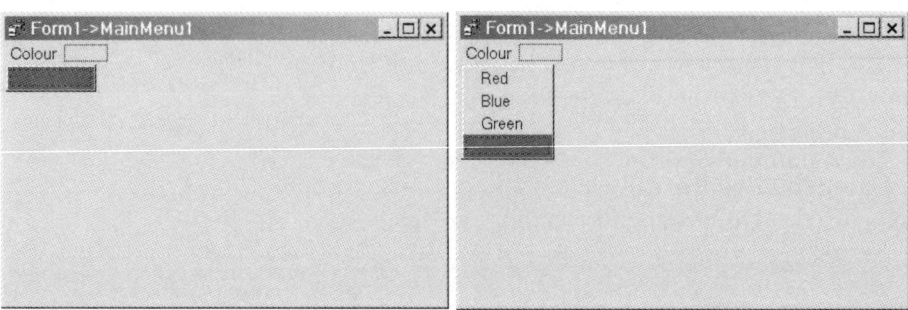

Enter "Red", then "Blue" and then "Green", pressing `Enter` each time. The Colour menu now has three selectable options as shown above (right). The blank 'box' at the bottom of a drop-down list in the menu editor does not appear in the program window. Run your program.

18

The program should compile and run successfully, displaying an empty form with a Colour menu. Clicking on `Colour` causes a drop-down menu offering the three options to appear. Any option may be selected but, of course, nothing happens as yet. Note that in the context of coding, a menu option is called a menu **item**.

- Close your program and return to the menu editor, by double-clicking on the menu icon on the form if necessary. Now press the right arrow key on the keyboard. The editor prepares for a second menu to the right of *Colour*. Type "Style" and give the Style menu the items (options) "Upper" and "Lower". The editor is waiting for a third item. Press the minus (-) key and then `Enter`. Now add a fourth item "Clear".

This has shown how you can build up any number of menus in the main menu of a program window. The effect of the minus key is to introduce a **separator** into a menu. Separators are used commonly to present menu items in associated groups. As you would probably guess, if you were to run the program at this stage, nothing new would happen except that you would now have two menus and more options to choose from. Before trying that, you should explore one further feature.

- Enter the menu editor and select "Colour". In the Object Inspector, change the caption "Red" to "Re&d", placing an ampersand before the 'd'. Run your program. Try the effect of pressing `Alt+C`, or `Alt` and then C. Now, while in the Colour menu, try pressing D.

In addition to now having a Style menu, you should have noticed the following. The 'C' of Colour is now shown underlined, as is the 'd' in Red. Pressing `Alt+C` or `Alt` and then C invokes the Colour menu. Then, pressing D causes the drop-down menu to vanish: this happens because there is no code in the event handler to invoke the option `Red`. (With an appropriate event handler, pressing D, once in the Colour menu, would invoke the `Red` menu item, as you will see below.)

Pressing `Alt` activates the menu system from anywhere in a program. In some versions of *Windows* the underlining does not appear until the `Alt` key is pressed.

What you have done here is to change the **shortcut for the menu item** Red from the default R to D. The effect of adding the ampersand to a menu item caption is to select the letter which follows it as the 'hotkey' for that menu item. At run-time, the hotkey letters are underlined; you will have observed this in Builder, for example.

- Close your program and return to the menu editor. Select the *Colour* item. If the Object Inspector is not visible, press `F11`. Notice that this component has been given the default name *Colour1*, and it has a list of properties, some of which will be familiar. Change the value of the *Enabled* property to **false**. Now locate the component with default name *Upper1* and change its *Enabled* property value to **false**. Run the program.

The default names given to menu items by Builder will usually be left unaltered. By default Builder makes the first letter of a menu item a shortcut key although nothing shows in the Object Inspector.

You should discover that the whole of the *Colour* menu, and the *Upper* item on the *Style* menu are disabled; they appear greyed out and cannot be selected. Each menu item has a number of properties which, as you have just done with the *Enabled* property, can be set from the Object Inspector. Each menu item has an event: *OnClick*. This event occurs when the user selects the menu items. To make something happen when a menu item is selected, some code is needed.

- Returning to the Form Designer, drop an edit box onto the form, and set its *Text* property to "Testing". Now return to the menu editor and double-click on the Red option in the Colour menu. The Code Editor opens and has created a template, in the form of an event handler called *Red1Click*, for selection of this option. Enter the code

  ```
  Form1->Color = clRed;
  ```

  In the same way, double-click on the Upper option in the Style menu and enter the code

  ```
  Edit1->Text = Edit1->Text.UpperCase();
  ```

  in the provided template for *Upper1Click*.

  Next, reset the value of the *Enabled* property of the components *Colour1* and *Upper1* to **true**. Run the program.

The program should run successfully, and now things *can* happen. Selection of the Red option changes the Form's colour to red, and selection of the Upper option converts the text in the edit box to upper case. You can add your own code to the other options if you wish to experiment further.

What these experiments have shown is that construction of menus to accompany forms is quite straightforward using the menu editor. As far as attaching event handler code is concerned, selection of options behaves in all respects just like button clicks, as you have worked with them in the previous unit.

# 3 Coding the design

The next stage is to build the form (the program's main window) using Builder's tools. Although this does not feel much like writing code, that is what will be happening in the background, so it is important to approach the task with a clear plan, just as you did when writing code by hand.

The overall plan for the program window (form) is that it will have:
o a main menu,
o an input area grouped using a panel,
o an output area consisting of a memo.

The next set of computer activities ask you to implement this basic visual design, and investigate some properties that enable different components to fit together neatly on a form.

**Computer Activity 3.1**

Start Builder and open a new application. You should save the project as `VisWH1`, in the `Block III` folder. (As you make subsequent changes, you should save your work from time to time.)

Drop a panel (*TPanel*) and a memo (*TMemo*) onto the form, and set the initial values of some properties according to the following property table.

| Type   | Identifier | Property  | Value          |
|--------|------------|-----------|----------------|
| *TForm*  | *WHForm*     | *Caption*   | Warehouse      |
|        |            | *Position*  | poScreenCenter |
| *TPanel* | *InputPanel* | *Caption*   | ""             |
| *TMemo*  | *OutputBox*  | *ReadOnly*  | true           |
|        |            | *Lines*     | ""             |

Use the *Name* property to set the values given in the identifier column.

As in *Unit 1*, in order to set the *Lines* property of *OutputBox* to be empty, you need to do the following:
o select *OutputBox* on the form;
o select the *Lines* property in the Object Inspector;
o click on the ellipsis (...) button to open the String list editor;
o use the backspace key to clear the editing window; click on the OK button.

(a) Run the new application and try resizing the window. What do you observe about the behaviour of the panel and memo components?

(b) Change the *Align* property of the panel component to `alTop`. Run the program again, and observe the behaviour of the panel and memo components when you resize the program window.

(c) Change the *Align* property of the memo component to `alClient`. Repeat the running and resizing experiment.

[*Solution on page 48*]

If you have the time, you may wish to discover the effect of different values of the *Align* property in the Help system. A quick way to do this is to click on the 'Align' property in the Object Inspector and press **F1**, which will call up the Help topic.

Setting the *Align* property appropriately is a useful tool in making sure that your visual designs behave as expected when resized by the user.

**Computer Activity 3.2**

Drop a MainMenu component onto the form and name it *MainMenu*. Open the menu editor and create two menus, as explained in Subsection 2.2:

○ a File menu with items Open, Save and (after a separator) Exit;
○ an Activity menu with items Delivery and Order.

The default shortcut is fine in each case except for 'Exit': it is a *Windows* convention to have 'x' as the shortcut to 'Exit'. Run your program to test that the menus appear correctly, by clicking on `File` and `Activity`, and also by using the shortcuts.

> Shortcut letters must be unique in any one menu item list; two identical underlined letters must not be visible and active at one time.

[*Solution on page 48*]

---

The final visual building stage, before adding code to event handlers, is to place the labels, edit boxes and buttons in the panel representing the data entry area.

**Computer Activity 3.3**

Place on the *InputPanel* component (in order from left to right) a label, an edit box, another label, another edit box and two buttons. Adjust their positions and sizes until you are happy with their appearance. (You may also wish to experiment with the *BevelInner* and *BevelOuter* properties of the *InputPanel* component, in order to improve its appearance.)

> Note that these edit boxes, labels and buttons have their *Enabled* property set to **true** by default.

Change the *Name*, *Caption* and *Text* (where appropriate) properties of the components just added. The *Name* and *Caption* properties should match the data table developed for this problem in Exercise 2.2. After these changes, you may wish to re-adjust sizes and positions of these components.

Run the new version of your program, and check that your changes are incorporated in the program window. Is it possible to type text into the memo?

[*Solution on page 48*]

---

The remaining tasks are coding event handlers for selection of menu items and clicking on buttons. If you look back to the design stages discussed earlier, you will find that some of the menu items do not communicate with the warehouse engine, they just clear edit boxes and set things up ready for input. The `File|Open`, `File|Save` menu items and `Accept` button all communicate with the warehouse and, in the case of the `Accept` button there are visual effects resulting from this communication. The coding will be completed in two stages: the visual effects first, then the effects that require communication with the warehouse.

## Computer Activity 3.4

Create the `File|Exit` event handler skeleton by, in the form designer, clicking on `File` and then clicking on `Exit`. Add the single statement

`Close();`

to the handler skeleton.

Run the new version of your program, and check that `File|Exit` does now close the program.

[*Solution on page 48*]

---

The design developed in Section 1 for the `Activity|Delivery` event handler is as follows.

`Activity|Delivery`

1. prepare data entry area
2. disable `Activity` menu
3. set form's caption to indicate "Delivery"
4. *IsDelivery* ← **true**

With the exception of the last step, which is not visual, this design can be coded using methods that you have investigated earlier. The last step will be incorporated when non-visual effects are coded later.

## Computer Activity 3.5

(a) Create the event handler skeleton for `Activity|Delivery` by double-clicking on this menu item in the menu editor. Add to it the following code which corresponds to steps 1 to 3 of the above design. The name of the menu item, which Builder calls `Activity1` by default, has been changed to the more informative `ActivityMenu`.

```
InputPanel->Enabled = true;
CodeBox->SetFocus();
ActivityMenu->Enabled = false;
WHForm->Caption = "Warehouse - Delivery";
```

Run your program and check that the event handler for the menu item `Activity|Delivery` behaves, visually, as planned.

*This way of creating event handlers is an alternative to that in the previous computer activity.*

*In code, a meaningful identifier is preferable. You will need to change the name of this menu item in the Object Inspector.*

(b) Now write the visual code for the `Activity|Order` event handler in a similar way. The design developed in Section 1 is as follows.

`Activity|Order`

1. prepare data entry area
2. disable `Activity` menu
3. set form's caption to indicate "Order"
4. *IsDelivery* ← **false**

Save and run the revised version of your project.

[*Solution on page 49*]

The click of the Accept button is to provoke a good deal of non-visual activity; the two edit boxes are read, their contents converted and sent to the warehouse engine for processing, and results of this processing displayed. You are not yet ready to write the non-visual code, but the rest can be written as below. Note how a comment and a dummy output message are used as markers for later code to be added.

```
//Processing code goes here.
OutputBox->Lines->Add("Results from processing");
CodeBox->Clear();
QuantityBox->Clear();
CodeBox->SetFocus();
```

You can add this code in the next activity, at the same time adding the code for the event handler for the Finished button click (which produces only visual effects).

## Computer Activity 3.6

Create the event handler skeleton for the Accept button (by double-clicking on it) and adding the code above. Create the event handler skeleton for the Finished button, and add code for the the event handler based on the design idea from Section 1. Run the revised version of your project.

[*Solution on page 49*]

---

In order to code the non-visual effects, two things must be done. First, the boolean variable *IsDelivery* must be declared and the assignments to it implemented as determined at the design stage. Second, the warehouse engine must be made available to the project and communicate with the interface. To avoid accidental modification of the definition of the *WareHouseType* class, only the header file (B3WHImpl.h) and pre-compiled library file (B3WHImpl.lib) have been made available.

## Computer Activity 3.7

With the file VisWH1U.cpp open in the Code Editor, right-click and select Open Source/Header File (or press Ctrl+F6) to open the header file. Add the line

```
bool IsDelivery;
```

to the **private** section of the *TWHForm* class declaration.

Add a line of code at the end of each of the event handlers for Activity|Delivery and Activity|Order to set *IsDelivery* correctly. Run the revised version of your project.

[*Solution on page 49*]

---

Having dealt with *IsDelivery*, attention turns to the engine.

## Computer Activity 3.8

Use `Project|Add to Project...` (or the green plus button) to add the file `B3WHImpl.lib` to the project. Add the line

```
#include "B3WHImpl.h"
```

to the file `VisWHU1.h` just before the start of the *TWHForm* class declaration. Declare an instance (*Warehouse*) of the class *WarehouseType* in the **private** section of the *TWHForm* declaration.

Save the latest version of your project, and check that it still runs as before.

[*Solution on page 49*]

---

The remaining code statements to be added to event handlers all use methods from the *WarehouseType* class definition.

The designs from Section 1 for `File|Open` and `File|Save` event handlers

1  *Warehouse.Init*("B3WHData.dat")

and

1  *Warehouse.Save*("B3WHData.dat")

are very simple! The `Accept` button event handler is rather more involved: the contents of each of the edit boxes has to be read and converted from a string to an integer.

In *Unit 1*, you used the *AnsiString* class method *ToInt* to convert a string to an integer. There is an alternative method, which will serve the present needs nicely. The *AnsiString* class method *ToIntDef* works in the same way as *ToInt*, but with the extra property that, if it cannot convert the string to an integer value, it returns a default value instead. The default is supplied as the parameter to the method. For example, if *s* is a string variable, then the statement

```
i = s.ToIntDef(0);
```

will set *i* to the result of converting *s* to an integer, or to zero if conversion fails for some reason. Equally,

```
Code = (CodeBox->Text).ToIntDef(0);
```

will take what the user typed into *CodeBox* and attempt to interpret it as an integer. *Code* will be set to this value if conversion succeeds or to zero if conversion fails.

In order to display strings in *OutputBox*, you will need to use the *Add* method of the *Lines* property mentioned earlier.

## Exercise 3.1

Code the following design for the `Accept` button event handler.

1      set *Code* to value obtained by converting string (or 0 on failure)
2      set *Quantity* to value obtained by converting string (or 0 on failure)
3      **if** *Code* > 0 **and** *Quantity* > 0 **then**
4.1        **if** *IsDelivery* **then**
4.2           display *Store(Code, Quantity)* in *OutputBox*
4.3        **else**
4.4           display *Supply(Code, Quantity)* in *OutputBox*
4.5        **ifend**
5      **ifend**
6      clear *Code* edit box
7      clear *Quantity* edit box
8      give focus to *Code* edit box

[*Solution on page 45*]

## Computer Activity 3.9

Add the code from the solution to Exercise 3.1 to the event handler for the `Accept` button. You will need to add declarations of the integer variables *Code* and *Quantity* to your code. They *could* be added in the **private** section of the *TWHForm* declaration, as *IsDelivery* was. However, unlike *IsDelivery*, they are needed only within the one event handler, so should be declared (locally) there.

*The dummy output message added earlier will need to be removed when this code is added.*

Run the revised version of your program. Choose `Activity|Delivery` and enter 1 in the code box and 10 in the quantity box. Press the `Accept` button. Repeat this sequence to attempt to deliver this amount of this product five times in all.

*You can use* `Tab` *key to move between the code box and the quantity box.*

[*Solution on page 50*]

The previous activity may or may not have been successful. The course team obtained results which varied according to the version of Builder used (two versions were used during course development) and operating system version. As suggested in the solution, what is required is proper, system-independent initialisation of the warehouse contents. The next computer activity explores this initialisation.

## Computer Activity 3.10

Create event handlers for the `File|Open` and `File|Save` menu items.

(a) Run the revised version of your program, and repeat the attempt to deliver several lots of 10 of product code 1 that you did previously. How do the results compare with those of the previous activity?

(b) Run the program again; this time, choose `File|Open` before attempting the delivery. Comment on the results.

[*Solution on page 50*]

The result of the last two activities shows that something is far from right. Yet the coding reflects the designs, and they appear correct. The problem is that something is missing. When procedural programs were discussed in

Blocks I and II, an early step in every design was the initialisation of all relevant variables. The design and coding for this problem has no such initialisation built in. It is not satisfactory to rely on the user remembering to use **File|Open** before doing any work; the initialisation should happen *automatically*. So, where should the initialisation happen? There is no obvious 'beginning' of a *Windows* project in Builder. As with all such issues, the answer lies in events.

The forms which provide the windows for programs have a number of events associated with them. One important event for initialisation purposes is the *OnCreate* event that occurs when the system constructs the window (but before it becomes visible on the screen). You can use a handler for this event to do any initialisation tasks except those (like setting the focus to some component) which require the window to be visible to make sense. In the case of the warehouse, it makes sense to call the *Init* method in the *OnCreate* event handler to ensure that the warehouse is properly initialised.

The state of the warehouse ought to be saved automatically when the program closes. Again, it is unwise to rely on the user remembering to do this. The *Save* method of the warehouse *could* be called in the **File|Exit** event handler. Since there are a number of ways that the program can be shut down, it is safer to incorporate the saving in another event. The event corresponding to *OnCreate* is *OnDestroy*. Rather than duplicate coding (even though each is only one line), you can make use of the fact that event handlers which do the right things already exist.

## Computer Activity 3.11

From the drop-down list at the top of the Object Inspector, select **WHForm**. Choose the **Events** tab. Click on **OnCreate** in the left-hand column and then use the drop-down list in the right-hand column to select *Open1Click*.

What you have just done is to make the event handler (called *Open1Click*) for the **File|Open** menu item into the event handler for the form's *OnCreate* event as well. Similarly, attach *Save1Click* (the **File|Save** event handler) to the form's *OnDestroy* event.

The event handler for **File|Open** contains a single statement involving the *Init* method, and that for **File|Save** contains a single statement involving the *Save* method.

Save and run the new version of your program, and test the new arrangement as follows.

(a) Choose **Activity|Delivery** and store 10 of product code 1 five times. This should succeed with appropriate messages displayed.

(b) Choose **Activity|Order** and attempt to request 30 of product code 1 three times. Appropriate location and shortfall messages should appear.

(c) Deliver 10 of product code 1 five times again. Close the program. Restart the program, and check that requesting 30 of product code 1 three times produces the same messages as before.

[*Solution on page 50*]

---

Whilst the completed program still has some rough edges, it is a reasonable first attempt at a *Windows*-based warehouse program. For example, a printed version of the contents of the output display really ought to be available. However, you have done enough on this problem to illustrate the basic steps in designing and implementing an interface to an existing class (here *WarehouseType*).

There is one possibility — pressing the `Finished` button for the last entry *without* first pressing the `Accept` button — which has been mentioned before, but really ought to be considered briefly. As things stand, this action would result in the last entry being lost. The responsibilty for not committing this error, which would probably be discovered in testing, could be left with the user, but it is simple enough to overcome. The `Finished` button event handler should include the code of the `Accept` button event handler *before* the code for its own tasks. (Note that, with this modification, no harm will be done if `Accept` has already been pressed, as there will be no data.)

In the next section, some of the Builder-generated code will be reviewed to show how features of object-oriented programming have been used.

# 4 Inheritance and wrapping

The visual warehouse program was built by adapting existing objects to carry out the task in hand. The code which Builder generated illustrates two ways of adapting objects: **inheritance** and **wrapping**.

*This is a reading section: there are no exercises or computer activities.*

The code also makes heavy use of **pointers**, or **pointer variables**, which were mentioned briefly in the previous unit. As you will see in this section, all variable declarations that Builder generates for visual components are pointer declarations.

To start with, here is part of the contents of CTVWH4U.h.

```
class TWHForm : public TForm
{
 __published: // IDE-managed Components
   TPanel *InputPanel;
   TMemo *OutputBox;
   ....
   TButton *AcceptButton;
   ....
   void __fastcall AcceptButtonClick(TObject *Sender);
   ...
 private: // User declarations
   bool IsDelivery;
   WarehouseType Warehouse;
 public: // User declarations
   ....
};
```

This is a standard C++ class definition, except for the **__published** and **__fastcall** keywords which are *Windows*-specific extensions to C++ added by Borland. The first line

```
class TWHForm : public TForm
```

is what makes inheritance work. It says that the new class (called *TWHForm*) is to **inherit** all the behaviour (fields, properties, methods, events, etc.) from the existing class *TForm*.

The effect of the **public** keyword in this line is to carry over to the new class the type of access (**public**, **private**, etc.) of the items in *TForm*.

The ancestor (*TForm*) is called the **base class**, and the new descendant class (*TWHForm*) is called the **derived class**.

*Derived classes are sometimes called subclasses. Since 'sub' carries a hint of having lesser abilities, the course team will not use this terminology.*

Inheritance is an extremely powerful tool. An instance of type *TForm* automatically has all the basic behaviour required of a window: the ability to close, be moved, minimised, resized, and so on. Thus, instances of the new *TWHForm* class have all these abilities too. When you added code to the *OnCreate* event handler (of *WHForm*, of type *TWHForm*) in the previous section, you were adding to the abilities inherited from *TForm* (which already does some standard things when the *OnCreate* event occurs).

The new class also *adds* to abilities inherited from *TForm* in another way. The declarations

```
TPanel *InputPanel;
TMemo *OutputBox;
```

mean that a *TWHForm* object will have two additional fields, compared to a *TForm* object. One is a pointer (*InputPanel*) to a *TPanel* component; the other is a pointer (*OutputBox*) to a *TMemo* component. Both *InputPanel* and *OutputBox* are pointers to objects: they are said to be **wrapped** in the new class *TWHForm*.

Such declarations add to any fields inherited from the base class.

There is a sharp difference between inheritance and wrapping. Because a *TWHForm* object is *descended* from a *TForm* object, it knows how to respond to, say, being resized without *any* new code being written. However, such an object does *not* know how to display string data, even though it has *wrapped* in it a *TMemo*. To display a string, you had to write code that explicitly asks the *TMemo* object to get the method *Add*, of its *Lines* property, to add a string.

Next, the way in which Builder adds visual components to your form is discussed. The reason that all visual components are handled via pointers is buried in the history of Borland's Visual Component Library. However, pointers have always been a feature of C and C$^{++}$ programming, so they merit a little discussion here.

Pointers were (originally) the address in the computer's memory where the variable concerned was stored. As memory management schemes have become more complex, this is no longer actually true, but it does no harm to think of a pointer in this way.

In a modern PC, the use of hard disk space to supplement RAM (amongst other issues) means that memory addressing is an involved business.

Different programming languages have different ways of indicating pointers. This course will use the C$^{++}$ notation in both design and code.

In C$^{++}$, the asterisk (∗) is used to indicate that pointers are being used. The syntax

```
*X
```

means 'that which *X* points to'. Thus, the declaration

```
TPanel *InputPanel;
```

means that *\*InputPanel* (that is, that which *InputPanel* points to) is of type *TPanel*. Simplifying this description a little leads to saying that *InputPanel* is a pointer to a *TPanel*. It is important to understand that
- *InputPanel* is a pointer to a *TPanel* object;
- *\*InputPanel* is the *TPanel* object itself.

In C$^{++}$, pointer declarations can be made without much regard to spacing. The following three declarations, with different spacings, all have identical effect.

```
TPanel *InputPanel;
TPanel * InputPanel;
TPanel* InputPanel;
```

The first has already been described. The course team sees little merit in the second form and will not use it. The third has some merit. If *TPanel\**

is read as being a new type: '*TPanel*-pointer', then it says *InputPanel* is a *TPanel*-pointer. Since the code generated automatically by Builder uses the first form, so will the course team.

In passing, it should be mentioned that pointers to *any* type can be declared. This course will use pointers only to objects, but you may meet pointers to integers or characters, say, elsewhere. Such pointers would be declared as follows.

```
int *PointerToInt;
char *PointerToChar;
```

It is not at all obvious at first why pointer variables are necessary. For what you have done so far, they are not! The only reason that they have appeared is that the Visual Component Library and Builder work with them. However, some of the class types that you *will* meet do require them for the following reason. Ordinary variables have to be decided upon (and declared) when the program is being written. You cannot decide that you need another string, say, whilst the program is running. That is embarrassing for the designer of the *TMemo* class because the amount of text in the memo window is beyond the programmer's control. The *Add* method of the *Lines* property of *TMemo* has to be able to add a number of lines that the programmer of the *TMemo* class cannot possibly predict. Should the *TMemo* design allow for the largest amount of text that Builder can handle? That is over 2 billion characters and most PCs would complain if asked to provide that much memory for a single variable! Pointers provide the solution to this problem because a pointer does not occupy much room (usually about the same as an integer) and C$^{++}$ has provisions for only allocating memory for the actual variable pointed to when it is needed. How variables can be 'declared' when the program is running will be discussed later in the block.

The use of pointers for objects has led to an additional way of referring to fields, methods, etc., within objects. You have already used the dot notation for accessing fields and methods when an object has been declared. If *o* is an object with a field *f*, then *o.f* is used to access that field. When pointers are used, you can use the same approach. If you have the (pointer) declaration

```
TMemo *Memo;
```

then the *Clear* method of the *TMemo* can be accessed as follows.

```
(*Memo).Clear();
```

(Read this as 'the *Clear* method of that which is pointed to by *Memo*'.)

However, it is more usual to use the arrow notation

> Some people find the arrow a useful reminder that they are dealing with a pointer.

```
Memo->Clear();
```

for this purpose.

This concludes the brief review of inheritance, wrapping and pointers that arise from the way that the visual warehouse program was coded. If you wish, you may want to look up *TMemo* in the Builder Help system. By investigating the `Hierarchy` link from the main *TMemo* Help page, you can see the chain of ancestors of the *TMemo* class. Following the `Properties`,

`Methods` and `Events` links will show you where in the ancestry each capability was added. You may well notice that the general principle is that a capability is added as early (high up) in the hierarchy as possible.

Much more could be written about both inheritance and pointers. What has been said here just gives some idea of what the code generated by Builder is doing. Pointers, in particular, will be discussed a little more, later in the course.

# 5 Multi-window designs

The single-window design for the warehouse interface was a fairly straight adaptation of the original console application version. It would be more convenient for the user if a multi-window approach had been adopted. This would allow the user to have several delivery and/or order windows open at one time, and permit the user to switch between windows as required. (Builder is a multi-window program, as are most word-processor packages.)

*In practice, a client is likely to specify an efficient, multi-task solution.*

The overall structure of such multi-window programs is that they have a **main window**, within which individual windows are created and destroyed as needed. The windows inside the main window are referred to as **child windows**. In this section, you are asked to modify the earlier design to fit a main window/child window approach. You will then be asked to code the resulting design. As well as some new design considerations, you will meet a number of new ideas concerned with implementing multi-window programs and some of the corresponding features of the Visual Component Library.

### Problem Specification   Multi-window Warehouse

Design and code an interface to the warehouse class, meeting the following specification.
- The main window should contain only a main menu at start-up.
- The user's options on this menu should be the same as in the previous interface.
- The current state of the warehouse should be loaded at start-up from the file `B3WHData.dat` if it is available.
- The current state should be saved at shut-down in the file `B3WHData.dat`.
- When the Delivery menu item is selected, a new child window should open for the input and output; it should be labelled to indicate that it belongs to a delivery.
- When the Order menu item is selected, a new child window should open for the input and output; it should be labelled to indicate that it belongs to an order.

- As many delivery or order child windows as required may be open simultaneously.
- The user should be able to close any individual delivery or order window, and this action should correspond to that of clicking on a `Finished` button.
- The individual delivery and order child windows should be based on the single window used in the earlier version (but lacking the main menu).

□

The final requirement is typical of such a revised interface specification. The reason for it is normally to avoid extensive retraining of users. Where the new interface has similar activities to the old one, the way the user carries them out should also be as similar as possible.

The solution to this problem will go through the usual stages: visual design, design for menu and button actions, designing the form(s) in Builder, and coding of actions (event handlers).

### Exercise 5.1
Sketch the appearance of the program main window before any child windows have been opened.

### Exercise 5.2
Sketch a suggested appearance of the program interface with one delivery and one order child window open.

[*Solutions on page 46*]

---

In the following exercises, you should break down your designs into as many of the three stages: visual effects before any data is processed, data processing effects and visual effects after data processing, as are relevant to the particular case.

### Exercise 5.3
Suggest designs, based on the solutions to Exercises 5.1 and 5.2, for what should happen when the user chooses (from the main menu)

(a) to process a delivery;

(b) to process an order.

### Exercise 5.4
What differences from the single window application, if any, do you envisage in the multi-windows application

(a) when the `Accept` button is pressed?

(b) when the `Finished` button is pressed?

[*Solutions on page 46*]

---

The design work has reached the stage where coding can be considered. The visual design of the program's main window is simpler than before, since it now has only a main menu—no labels, panels, edit boxes, buttons or memos. There is one change: the window must 'know' that it is supposed to act as a container for a number of child windows.

In *Windows*-speak, multi-window programs of the type being discussed are known as **MDI applications**. The letters MDI stand for **M**ultiple **D**ocument **I**nterface, reflecting the fact that such programs first appeared for working with text documents.

In the following activities you will start to code the multi-windows program. Much of what you will need to do will be the same as for the single-window program. This will provide you with the chance to consolidate the various coding techniques covered in earlier sections.

### Computer Activity 5.1

Start Builder (if necessary) and open a new application. Save the project using the name `VisWH2U1.cpp` for the first file (the form file) and `VisWH2.bpr` for the project name, in the `Block III` folder.

Drop a main menu onto the form and name it *MainMenu*. Use the menu editor to create File and Activity menus and their drop-down menus. Add ampersand (`&`) characters to associate shortcut keys with menu items as you did in Section 3. Change the properties of the form as follows.

| Type  | Identifier | Property                        | Value                                        |
|-------|-----------|---------------------------------|----------------------------------------------|
| *TForm* | *WHMain*  | *Position* *FormStyle* *Caption* | poScreenCenter fsMDIForm MDI Warehouse |

Use the Help system to discover the significance of the value *fsMDIForm* for the *FormStyle* property of the class *TForm*.

Save, run and test run your program.

### Computer Activity 5.2

This activity adds the warehouse files to the project and deals with those coding issues that affect only the main form.

Add the file `B3WHImpl.lib` to the project, and add a line to include `B3WHImpl.h` near the top of the file `VisWH2U1.h`. Add

```
WarehouseType Warehouse;
```

to the **public** section of the *TWHMain* class declaration. Create event handlers for each of the items on the `File` menu in turn, adding the same code as you did in Computer Activities 3.4 and 3.10.

The declaration of *Warehouse* has to be **public** this time because objects outside the main form, namely the child windows, will need access to the warehouse object.

The event handlers *OnCreate* and *OnDestroy* should be dealt with at this stage. These event handlers are to cause automatic loading of the warehouse from the file and saving to the file, respectively.

(a) How can writing code for the *OnCreate* and *OnDestroy* event handlers be avoided?

Implement the solution to part (a).

(b) Check, by running it, that the revised version of the program still compiles correctly.

[*Solutions on page 51*]

The next stage is to design the form that will be used for the child windows, that is, for actually handling the processing. The next activity deals with the visual design stage of this form. The question of how to make various copies of it appear as required will be tackled afterwards.

You may have some difficulty locating the form that you wish to work with, once you have two or more forms (and corresponding code files) involved in your project. You may find View|Forms... or the View Form speed button (three to the left of the Run one) useful: either produces a list of forms in the current project, from which you can select the one on which you wish to work by double-clicking. Also recall that clicking on F12 is useful for switching between code for a form and the form designer.

## Computer Activity 5.3

From the Builder menu choose File|New Form and immediately choose File|Save giving the filename VisWH2U2.cpp when prompted. (This file name is chosen because it is the second unit belonging to this project.) You have now created a second form as part of the project. Set property values for this form as follows. (Remember also to set the *Name* property from the identifier column.)

*Make sure that it is saved to the correct folder.*

| Type | Identifier | Property | Value |
|---|---|---|---|
| *TWHChild* | *WHChild* | *FormStyle* | fsMDIChild |
|  |  | *Caption* | "" |

Following the procedures that you used in Section 3, place a panel (for input) and a memo (for output) on the new form. On the panel place two labels, two edit boxes and two buttons so as to implement the visual design for the child form illustrated in the solution to Exercise 5.2.

Set the properties of the various components as follows.

| Type | Identifier | Property | Value |
|---|---|---|---|
| *TPanel* | *InputPanel* | *Caption* | "" |
|  |  | *Align* | alTop |
| *TLabel* | *CodeLabel* | *Caption* | Code |
| *TLabel* | *QuantityLabel* | *Caption* | Quantity |
| *TEdit* | *CodeBox* | *Text* | "" |
|  |  | *TabOrder* | 0 |
| *TEdit* | *QuantityBox* | *Text* | "" |
| *TButton* | *AcceptButton* | *Caption* | Accept |
| *TButton* | *FinishedButton* | *Caption* | Finished |
| *TMemo* | *OutputBox* | *Lines* | "" |
|  |  | *Align* | alClient |

*Setting TabOrder to zero for CodeBox gives this box initial focus.*

(a) Save and run the program. What do you observe? Close the program.

(b) Run the program again, and this time attempt to close the child window by clicking on the cross icon in its top right-hand corner. What happens? Close the program.

The default behaviour of the MDI child window is not quite what is wanted. To make it close instead of minimise, the default *OnClose* event handler has to be modified. To do so, select the child form in the Object Inspector and then the Events tab. Double-click on the right-hand column of the *OnClose* event to create the event handler skeleton. Add a single line of code as follows.

`Action = caFree;`

(The significance of this statement will be discussed shortly.)

(c) Run the program again. Can the child window now be closed?

[*Solution on page 52*]

---

There are two things obviously missing from the solution so far: a child window opens automatically when the program starts, and there is no way (yet) of creating extra child windows. In fact, there is a third difficulty — the child window as designed has no way of 'knowing' whether it is supposed to be a delivery-processing window or an order-processing window. These three problems will be dealt with in order.

The default behaviour of Builder-constructed programs is to create any windows that belong to the project when the program is run. Builder refers to this as **auto-creation**. The child windows in the present task are not wanted until the user selects the `Activity` menu, so they should not be auto-created. Windows can be removed from the list of those to be auto-created by using the `Project|Options...` menu item in Builder; you will do this in the next computer activity.

> The shortcut for this menu item is `Shift+Ctrl+F11`.

The second problem is solved by a C++ statement associated with the use of pointer variables. As mentioned earlier, declaring a pointer variable reserves memory only for the pointer, not the object that it points to. In order to have the pointer actually point to something useful, the **new** keyword is used. The way in which it will be needed for the Warehouse problem illustrates the general form. If a pointer to a `WHChild` object is declared by

> If you inspect the header file `VisWH2U2.h`, you will see that Builder has called the *class* involved `TWHChild`.

`TWHChild *Child;`

then the statement

`Child = new TWHChild(this);`

creates a new object of type *TWHChild* and sets *Child* to point to the newly created object. The parameter **this** is needed because visual objects need an **owner**. In the case of the child windows, the owner is, reasonably enough, the main window in which they appear. The creation of child windows will take place in an event handler for the menu of the main window. Within the main window, the keyword **this** represents the main window object. Thus, the C++ statement above does the necessary creation and setting of the owner for the child window.

The significance of setting *Action* to *caFree* earlier can now be explained. The C++ statement that destroys the object *Child* created with **new** is '`delete Child;`'; this has the effect of *freeing* the memory allocated for that object.

36

The effect of

```
Action = caFree;
```

in the *OnClose* event handler is to say that the object should be removed by using `delete` when the user requests that it be closed. (The delete statement does not have to be entered manually.)

The final problem is really the easiest. An idea from the single-window solution is adopted: a boolean variable *IsDelivery* can be added to the `public` part of the child window definition.

With these discussions in mind, designs for the `Activity|Delivery` and `Activity|Order` actions can be written. (When the Delivery (or Order) window first appears it will be in the initial state of child windows so, for example, the edit boxes will be clear of text, and *CodeBox* will have focus, since its *TabOrder* property has been set to zero.)

> The **private** section will not do as this would mean that it can be referenced only from within the child window. Since some of the main window's methods need to access the variable *IsDelivery*, the public section is appropriate.

`Activity|Delivery`

1. create new child window
2. set the child window *Caption* to "Delivery"
3. set *IsDelivery* to **true**

Except for the values of *Caption* and *IsDelivery*, the same design will do for orders.

## Computer Activity 5.4

Select `Project|Options...` from the main menu and choose the `Forms` tab in the resulting dialog box. Select `WHChild` in the `Auto-create forms:` list box, and drag it to the `Available forms:` list box. Click on `OK` to close the dialog box.

(a) Run the new version of your program, and check that no child window appears when the program starts. Close the program.

Open the header file `VisWH2U2.h` and add the declaration of the boolean variable *IsDelivery*, as suggested above. Create the event handler skeleton for the menu item `Activity|Delivery` and add the following code in it.

```
TWHChild *DeliveryForm;   //DeliveryForm points to an object of type TWHChild
   DeliveryForm = new TWHChild(this);
   DeliveryForm->Caption = "Warehouse - Delivery";
   DeliveryForm->IsDelivery = true;
```

Note the explicit use of `DeliveryForm->` to make sure that the properties of the correct form are set. Add an appropriately modified version of this code to implement the event handler for selection of the `Activity|Order` menu item.

(b) Run your program. What happens?

(c) Add an appropriate include statement to correct the error and try again.

[*Solution on page 52*]

The final stage in this project is to make the child windows actually do something, and to achieve that you have to implement the designs for the Accept and Finished buttons.

The code is in VisWH1U1.cpp.

**Computer Activity 5.5**

Create the event handler skeleton for the Accept button in the child windows. Enter the following code. As it is similar to the corresponding code in the previous version of the program, you may wish to cut and paste from there. (Since child windows are the context here, the lines for the *Store* and *Supply* methods must include WHMain->.)

```
int Code;
int Quantity;
Code = (CodeBox->Text).ToIntDef(0);
Quantity = (QuantityBox->Text).ToIntDef(0);
if ((Code > 0) && (Quantity > 0 ))
  if (IsDelivery)
  {
    OutputBox->Lines->Add(WHMain->Warehouse.Store(Code, Quantity));
  }
  else
  {
    OutputBox->Lines->Add(WHMain->Warehouse.Supply(Code, Quantity));
  }
CodeBox->Clear();
QuantityBox->Clear();
CodeBox->SetFocus();
```

(a) Predict an error that would be reported if you tried to compile the project in its current state. How should the error be prevented?

(b) Implement the Finished button click event handler.

(c) Run and test the latest version of your project. Verify that you can work with several order windows and several delivery windows open at one time, switching between them at will. (You may need to 'move' a window to reveal ones hidden underneath.)

[*Solution on page 52*]

---

This activity concludes the main work for this unit. As with the single-window interface coded earlier in the unit, there are some features that should be added. The main one is giving the user the option to choose the file that is used for loading and saving the warehouse state. The course team has chosen not to include this here because doing so raises a number of ancillary points that would have been a distraction from the main work. For example, the automatic loading on start-up would be more complex, and would have to force the user to choose a file (via a *Windows* file dialog box) before anything else could be done. The interface object (the main form in the case of the multi-window version) would have to keep a record of the current file name in use. The File menu would need both Save and Save As... items. Taken all round, the simpler approach here seemed preferable. The penalty, as was observed at the time, was slight inconvenience in some stages of testing.

A more minor point is that new child windows are created exactly on top of each other. To avoid this, you might like to try the effect of adding the line

`Cascade();`

to the `Activity|Delivery` and `Activity|Order` event handlers.

*It is possible that the child windows are cascaded by default on some systems.*

There are a number of questions raised by the way the second interface to the warehouse was constructed. A serious one is that each of the pointer variables *DeliveryForm* and *OrderForm* was declared inside the event handler that created it. Once a child was created (and the event handler finished executing) that variable no longer exists, so there is a child window which has, apparently, no way of being accessed because the pointer to it has been discarded. Generally speaking, discarding pointers without deleting the objects to which they point is a very bad idea. The memory occupied by the objects cannot be recovered and available memory gradually 'leaks' away. Commercial programs have been known to suffer from memory leaks; they cause great problems to users. Fortunately, no such leaks will happen in this case. When the child window was created as a child of the main form, the main form acquired a pointer to the child. (The pointer is contained in the property *MDIChildren* of a form with *FormStyle* set to *fsMDIForm*. Such windows keep a list of child windows automatically as they are created. The destruction of child windows that are finished with is done by the default actions of the main form's *OnDestroy* event handler. The main window tracks creation and destruction of child windows, so it always knows how many children it has and which one is active.)

The next unit will develop inheritance and wrapping as ways of adapting classes from a library to solve particular problems.

# Objectives

After studying this unit, you should be able to:

o design and code visual interfaces (single window or multi-window, as appropriate) to existing objects, setting initial values using the Object Inspector;

o design and code visual effects of, and processing code for, event handlers of button clicks and menu item selections, paying particular attention to set focus to, disable and enable appropriate components;

o apply the MT262 ground rules for *Windows* programming given in the Appendix;

o constuct a simple main menu with several menus having drop-down menus, making use of separators and programmer-defined shortcuts to menu items;

o declare variables in files and sections of files appropriate to their use;

o be aware of the need for proper initialisation and saving of data, making use of the event handlers *OnCreate* and *OnDestroy*;

o use the Borland Help system to investigate properties, events and methods of a given class;

o be aware of the roles of inheritance and wrapping in code generated by Builder when objects are adapted;

o identify pointer declarations in code;

o use and understand the use of the following terms: instance of a class, inheritance, wrapping, pointer, MDI application, child window.

# Appendix: Conventions

## Ground rules for *Windows* programs

The following ground rules give an indication of the *Windows* conventions adopted in MT262. You might wish to add to the list as you progress through the rest of the course.

- With very few exceptions, all programs have a main menu with at least one menu item. *You will meet one such exception in Block IV.*
- Every action that the user might wish to take is available by selecting from menus and submenus.
- Actions that are likely to be required frequently *may* be provided via buttons *as well as* menus.
- `Alt+character` keyboard shortcuts to menu headings and single-key shortcut to drop-down menu items should be indicated by underlining the chosen character on menus and buttons. Conventions such as 'F' for 'File' and 'x' for 'Exit' should be observed in these programmer-defined shortcuts.
- Standard tasks (cutting, copying, pasting) should always use the standard keyboard shortcuts in addition to programmer-defined shortcuts. Thus `Ctrl+C` should always be used for copying, where provided, and not some other shortcut peculiar to the program being written.
- Where standard menus (`File`, `Edit`, etc.) appear, they should do so in the order used by other *Windows* programs.

## Borland naming conventions

As you develop your use of the Builder toolkit, you may well notice that a number of the values that properties of components may take have slightly curious names. For example, the options for the *Position* property of a form are *poDesigned*, *poDefault* and so on: they are all prefixed *po* (for *po*sition). There are a number of such property values and the following table lists the ones that you are likely to use most often.

| Property | Prefix | Example | Comment |
|---|---|---|---|
| *Position* | *po* | *poScreenCenter* | Note American spelling |
| *BorderStyle* | *bs* | *bsDialog* | Sets outline of window |
| *BorderIcons* | *bi* | *biMaximize* | Sets which icons appear in the window's title bar |
| *Color* | *cl* | *clWhite* | Sets colour of window |
| *Cursor* | *cr* | *crDefault* | Sets appearance of mouse cursor when positioned over window |
| *FormStyle* | *fs* | *fsNormal* | Form is not an MDI window |
| *WindowState* | *ws* | *wsMaximized* | Form appears maximised |
| *ModalResult* | *mr* | *mrOk* | Result produced by pressing buttons |

# Solutions to the Exercises

## Section 1

### Solution 1.1

Taking the various menu options in order, it is possible to describe what each should do.

File|Open   Initialise the warehouse contents from a suitable data file. (The possibility of offering the user the option to choose the file used will be discussed later.)

File|Save   Save the current contents of the warehouse to a suitable data file. (See comment on previous item.)

File|Exit   Cause the program to stop running.

Activity|Delivery   Ask the user for the codes and quantities of items being delivered, and display a list of places to store them (or error message).

Activity|Order   Ask the user for the codes and quantities of items requested, and display a list of locations from which to collect them (or error message).

### Solution 1.2

The user has to have some way of entering the codes and quantities of the products being delivered or ordered—that is, there has to be a 'data entry area'. There also has to be some way of displaying the list of locations for storing or collecting goods—that is, there must be a 'results area'.

### Solution 1.3

In addition to providing names and captions (where appropriate) for the various components and menu items, the following initial properties would be set.

Initially, both edit boxes and both buttons should be disabled as the user should not be able to use them until a delivery or order activity has been chosen.

> Just how this is done in this case will be discussed in Section 3.

The two edit boxes and the results area should be empty of text. Also the user should not be able to make entries in the results area, that is, it should be 'read only'.

All the menu options will be enabled, by default, unless you opt to disable any. Having them all enabled is probably safe, though this decision might be reviewed when the exact way in which loading and saving the warehouse information is dealt with. For example, the information may be automatically loaded from a file when the program starts; but if not, then the saving option should probably be disabled until something has been loaded.

### Solution 1.4

Selection of the Activity|Order menu option should prepare the data entry area exactly as for a delivery. The only difference now is that the form's caption should indicate that it is an order being processed.

## Solution 1.5

In preparation for the start of the next activity, the data in the edit boxes and in the output display should be cleared.

## Solution 1.6

4    *IsDelivery* ← **false**

## Solution 1.7

The information returned by the *Supply* method has to be displayed, so 'else' step is as given below.

4.3   **else**
4.4       display *Supply*(*Code*, *Quantity*)
4.5   **ifend**

## Solution 1.8

The top-level design is as follows.

```
Finished
```

1    clear *Code* edit box
2    clear *Quantity* edit box
3    clear results area
4    enable `Activity` menu
5    disable components in data entry area
6    set form's caption back to "Warehouse"

If the user could be relied upon always to click the `Accept` button before the `Finished` button, there would be no need for clearing edit boxes here. This point will be revisited briefly later in the unit.

## Solution 1.9

Each design requires only a single step.

1    *Warehouse.Init*("B3WHData.dat")

1    *Warehouse.Save*("B3WHData.dat")

## Solution 1.10

The data file `B3WHData.dat` ought to be updated to reflect the changes to the warehouse state caused by deliveries and orders processed. It may be unwise to rely on the operator remembering to do `File|Save` before closing the program, so a save operation could be done automatically before closing.

Some programs simply warn the operator that changes ought to be saved and offer the choice of saving or not. You have probably met this type of behaviour with word-processing programs. (Builder behaves in this way.) Where security and/or accounting issues arise, it might be felt that changes *must* be recorded, whether the operator wants to or not! As usual with such decisions, there is no one 'right' answer for all programs.

# Section 2

## Solution 2.1

(a) Untangling the descriptions of the two classes suggests that the main difference is that *TRichEdit* handles rich text; that is, different parts of the text can have different properties such as bold, or italic, etc. The warehouse program does not really need this facility.

(b) The *TRichEdit* class has a *Print* method, but the *TMemo* class does not. This existence of such a method means that you would not have to write your own code for sending the contents of the component to the printer. Whilst an object from the *TMemo* class would be adequate for everything discussed so far, looking ahead to adding a print facility suggests that *TRichEdit* should at least be considered.

## Solution 2.2

The completed table is as follows. (You may have used different identifiers.)

| Type | Identifier | Description |
| --- | --- | --- |
| *TMainMenu* | *MainMenu* | Main menu for the program window |
| *TLabel* | *CodeLabel* | Label for product code box |
| *TLabel* | *QuantityLabel* | Label for product quantity box |
| *TEdit* | *CodeBox* | Input box for product code |
| *TEdit* | *QuantityBox* | Input box for product quantity |
| *TButton* | *AcceptButton* | Press to accept data in boxes |
| *TButton* | *FinishedButton* | Press to stop processing |
| *TMemo* | *OutputBox* | Displays information from warehouse object |
| *TPanel* | *InputPanel* | Groups data entry area items |

## Solution 2.3

In each case, the *Name* property and the *Caption* property (where applicable) will need changing from the default values given by Builder. The default names *could* be used, but will not lead to very readable code.

Since the components of a panel are disabled when the panel itself is disabled and since in this case all the components in the data entry area are disabled together (see the **Finished** button event handler, for example), the *Enabled* property of the *TPanel* object should certainly be used, on the grounds of efficiency.

Any enabling and disabling of the *TLabel* and *TButton* objects will be handled as part of the panel. No further properties of these two classes can be identified as being significant.

The *TEdit* boxes do not have a caption, and the *Enabled* property will not be needed for the same reasons as for the buttons. The *Text* property contains what is typed in by the user, so this property will certainly be needed. Amongst the methods, the *Clear* one is going to be useful in implementing the designs discussed. In addition, during design it was suggested that the Code box should be given focus at appropriate times. For this purpose the *SetFocus* method (which all visual components possess) will be useful.

Bearing in mind that the *TMemo* will be used only for output, and that the user should not be allowed to type into it, the *ReadOnly* property looks useful. The *TMemo* Help entry does not reveal any obvious way of adding a line of text to what is displayed. The *Lines* property holds the textual content of the memo, but how do you add another line to what is there? The clue is that *Lines* turns out to be an object of type *TStrings*. Following the trail reveals that *TStrings* represent a list of strings, and such objects do have a method, called *Add*, for adding a string to the end of the list.

The following table summarises the properties and methods that are likely to be useful in coding.

| Object | Property | Method |
|---|---|---|
| *TLabel* | *Caption* | |
| | *Name* | |
| *TPanel* | *Caption* | |
| | *Name* | |
| | *Enabled* | |
| *TButton* | *Caption* | |
| | *Name* | |
| *TEdit* | *Text* | *Clear* |
| | *Name* | *SetFocus* |
| *TMemo* | *Name* | *Clear* |
| | *ReadOnly* | *SetFocus* |
| | *Lines* | |
| *TStrings* | | *Add* |
| (*Lines* of *TMemo*) | | |

# Section 3

## Solution 3.1

Most of the design translates fairly easily. The only slightly verbose statements are concerned with displaying the strings returned by warehouse methods in *OutputBox*. For example, when attempting to store something, the string is

```
Warehouse.Store(Code, Quantity);
```

so displaying this requires the following statement.

```
OutputBox->Lines->Add(Warehouse.Store(Code, Quantity));
```

The complete code for the **Accept** button event handler is as follows.

```
Code = (CodeBox->Text).ToIntDef(0);
Quantity = (QuantityBox->Text).ToIntDef(0);
if ((Code > 0) && (Quantity > 0 ))
   if (IsDelivery)
   {
     OutputBox->Lines->Add(Warehouse.Store(Code, Quantity));
   }
   else
   {
     OutputBox->Lines->Add(Warehouse.Supply(Code, Quantity));
   }
CodeBox->Clear();
QuantityBox->Clear();
CodeBox->SetFocus();
```

# Section 5

## Solution 5.1

The course team solution is based on the original design but with the input and output areas removed, since they will belong to the individual child windows.

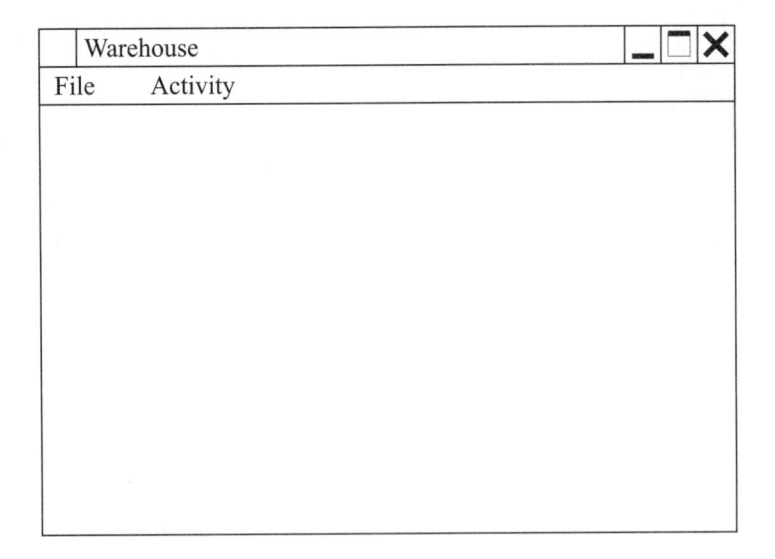

```
┌─────────────────────────────────────────┬─□×┐
│    Warehouse                            │   │
├─────────────────────────────────────────┴───┤
│ File    Activity                            │
│                                             │
│                                             │
│                                             │
│                                             │
│                                             │
│                                             │
│                                             │
│                                             │
└─────────────────────────────────────────────┘
```

## Solution 5.2

Each child window requires the same input and output components as the main window of the original design. This suggests that the appearance with two child windows might well be as follows.

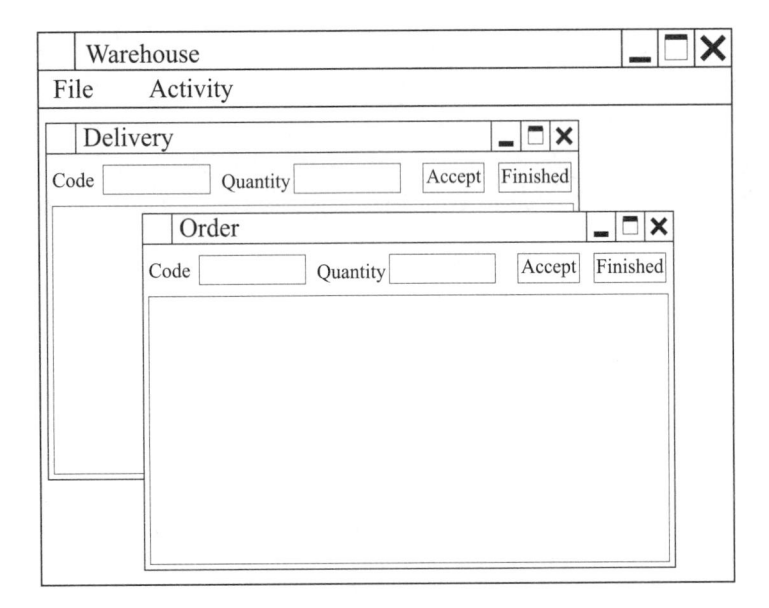

```
┌─────────────────────────────────────────┬─□×┐
│    Warehouse                            │   │
├─────────────────────────────────────────┴───┤
│ File    Activity                            │
│  ┌──────────────────────────────┬─□×┐       │
│  │ Delivery                     │   │       │
│  │ Code [    ] Quantity [    ] Accept Finished│
│     ┌──────────────────────────────┬─□×┐   │
│     │ Order                        │   │   │
│     │ Code [  ] Quantity [    ] Accept Finished│
│     │                                    │   │
│     │                                    │   │
│     │                                    │   │
│     └────────────────────────────────────┘   │
└─────────────────────────────────────────────┘
```

## Solution 5.3

(a) A new delivery window should appear ready for use. Expanding this description a little gives the following design.

    1    create new window
    2    set window caption to "Delivery"

(b) Except for the value of the caption, the design can be exactly the same as in part (a).

## Solution 5.4

(a) There are no differences envisaged. As before, the contents of the edit boxes have to be read and converted, the *Store* or *Supply* method of the warehouse — as appropriate — called and the returned string displayed. The edit boxes should then be prepared for the next entry.

(b) In the single window application, clicking the `Finished` button caused the `Activity` menu item to be enabled and the input panel to be disabled. Neither of these should happen now. The `Activity` menu is to be permanently enabled, since any number of activities are allowed simultaneously. The input panel appears (as part of the child window) only when an activity has been selected, so there is no need to disable it.

The only task that remains for the `Finished` button is to close the child window (whether it be delivery or order).

# Solutions to the Computer Activities

## Section 3

### Solution 3.1

(a) You should find that the panel and memo remain at their design size as the window is resized, that is, they do not change to match the main window.

(b) When you set the new value of *Align*, the panel should have moved to occupy the whole of the top edge of the main ('client') area of the form. When the new version is run, the panel resizes to remain in position at the top of the window, but the memo is still a fixed size.

(c) Changing the *Align* property of the memo should have caused the memo to occupy the whole of the remaining area of the form. When run, the panel and memo both resize themselves if the main window is resized.

### Solution 3.2

Clicking on `File`, or equivalently pressing `Alt+F`, causes the drop-down menu to appear. Selecting an option at this stage causes the drop-down menu to disappear (since there is no code in the event handler for this event).

Similar remarks apply to the `Activity` menu.

The course team version of the project is `CTVWH1.bpr`.

Did you notice in the Object Inspector that the separator is given the default name *N1*?

### Solution 3.3

The labels and buttons require their captions and names to be changed. Each edit box needs its name setting and its *Text* property set to blank, so that it appears empty.

You cannot type into the memo, since its *ReadOnly* property has been set to true.

The course team version of the project is `CTVWH2.bpr`.

### Solution 3.4

The only likely cause of any problem is incorrect spelling of the `Close` method.

## Solution 3.5

(a) You should have checked, in particular, that selecting Activity|Delivery causes 'Warehouse - Delivery' to appear, and that the cursor appears in the *CodeBox* edit box (the left-hand edit box). In addition, the Activity menu is now disabled.

(b) The only difference this time is the value of *Caption* of *WHForm*. (In the non-visual code, to be considered later, *IsDelivery* should be set to **false**.) The visual coding is as before. Note that *CodeBox* is still set as the active component.

The code for the Activity|Order menu item event handler is as follows.

```
InputPanel->Enabled = true;
CodeBox->SetFocus();
ActivityMenu->Enabled = false;
WHForm->Caption = "Warehouse - Order";
```

## Solution 3.6

The code for the Finished button click event handler is as follows.

```
CodeBox->Clear();
QuantityBox->Clear();
OutputBox->Clear();
ActivityMenu->Enabled = true;
InputPanel->Enabled = false;
Caption = "Warehouse";
```

You can check the functioning of the Accept button by entering a number in *CodeBox*, say, and then pressing it. You can check also that the enabling/disabling switch between the Activity menu and the input panel functions as intended.

Note that when the input panel is disabled, its components are not greyed out. This is a slight disadvantage when compared to disabling the components individually, which does result in greying out.

## Solution 3.7

The two lines to be added are:

```
IsDelivery = true;
```

in the Activity|Delivery menu item event handler and

```
IsDelivery = false;
```

in the Activity|Order menu item event handler.

## Solution 3.8

No code has been added, so there should be no errors.

The course team version of the project at this stage is CTVWH3.bpr.

## Solution 3.9

The variable declarations are as follows.

```
int Code;
int Quantity;
```

They should appear before the code from the solution to Exercise 3.1.

If you were careful about spelling, brackets and upper/lower-case letters, the revised version should compile and run.

With the suggested entries, what *should* happen is that messages saying where to place the successive delivery items should appear. The first in row 1, slot 1, then row 1, slot 2, and so on.

What may have happened was that a message
"Sorry, error storing product."
appeared, either immediately or after one or two presses.

The first situation arose because automatic initialisation of the warehouse state to zeros had taken place, but such initialisation cannot be relied upon (it is system dependent). The error message in the second case arose because such initialisation had not taken place. A proper initialisation procedure is called for; this is discussed in the main text following Computer Activity 3.10.

## Solution 3.10

(a) The event handler code for File|Open is

```
Warehouse.Init("B3WHData.dat");
```

and that for File|Save is as follows.

```
Warehouse.Save("B3WHData.dat");
```

Just adding the new event handlers should make no difference to the behaviour. It should be exactly the same, successful or not, as for Computer Activity 3.9.

(b) The File|Open event handler initialises the warehouse (from a file if one is available, or to empty if not). The deliveries should now succeed with the expected messages, regardless of what happened in earlier attempts.

## Solution 3.11

(a) The messages the course team received were as follows.

```
Store in row 1, slot 1
Store in row 1, slot 2
Store in row 1, slot 3
Store in row 1, slot 4
Store in row 1, slot 5
```

(b) On requesting the order specified, the messages for the three requests were as follows.

```
Take 10 from row 1, slot 1
Take 10 from row 1, slot 2
Take 10 from row 1, slot 3

Take 10 from row 1, slot 4
Take 10 from row 1, slot 5
Shortfall of 10

Shortfall of 30
```

(c) The messages were the same as indicated above, even with a program shut-down between delivery and order activities. This indicates that the warehouse data is being saved at shut-down and restored at start-up.

The final course team version of this project is `CTVWH4.bpr`.

# Section 5

### Solution 5.1

The *FormStyle* property being set to *fsMDIForm* is the signal that this form is to have additional abilities appropriate to acting as a container for other forms.

You should have found that the drop-down menus appear on selecting `File` and `Activity`. Did you remember to include the separator before `Exit`?

### Solution 5.2

You should have used `Project|Add to Project...` (or the green plus button) for the first task. The required line to include the header file is the following.

`#include "B3WHImpl.h"`

Clicking on the required drop-down menu item creates the event handler skeleton. The code lines are

`Warehouse.Init("B3WHData.dat");`

`Warehouse.Save("B3WHData.dat");`

`Close();`

for `File|Open`, `File|Save` and `File|Exit`, respectively.

(a) The events cause the same actions as `File|Open` and `File|Save`, so the *Events* tab in the Object Inspector can be used to link the events to the existing event handlers *OnCreate* and *OnDestroy*. (See Computer Activity 3.11.)

(b) Your program should run with no problems. The likely causes of any errors are: misspellings, omitting semicolons and omitting function brackets in `Close()`.

## Solution 5.3

(a) As well as the program's main form, a child window opens and is contained within the main window area.

(b) Instead of closing, the child window minimises within the main window.

(c) The addition made to the *OnClose* event handler should make the child window close instead of minimise when its cross icon is clicked.

The course team version of the project at this stage is `CTMDI1.bpr`.

## Solution 5.4

(a) Removing the child form from the list of automatically created forms has had the desired effect.

(b) There should be a number of error messages. Essentially, they all refer to the fact that the compiler does not know about the child windows when it is compiling `VisWH2U1.cpp`. To solve this, the line

```
#include "VisWH2U2.h"
```

is needed near the top of `VisWH2U1.cpp`.

(c) With the change just indicated, the project should now compile and run. No child windows should open initially (as they are no longer auto-created), but the `Activity|Deliver` and `Activity|Order` menu items should cause child windows to be created.

## Solution 5.5

(a) The information about *Warehouse* is not available because the appropriate `#include` statement has not been put in the code file for the child windows. The remedy is to place the line

*Warehouse* needs to be declared under `public` in `VisWH2U1.h`.

```
#include "VisWH2U1.h"
```

near the top of `VisWH2U2.cpp`, so that the child window code knows about the public object *Warehouse* in the *TWHMain* class.

(b) The `Finished` button does no more than close the child window. This can be achieved by placing the statement

```
Close();
```

in the event handler skeleton.

(c) The course team version of the complete project is available as `CTMDI2.bpr`. If your project fails to behave as expected, you may wish to compare your files with the corresponding ones in the course team version.

When several order (or delivery) windows are open simultaneously, you will have noticed that they all look the same. It would be convenient for the user to be able to distinguish between such windows by numbering them, say. This can be achieved, with some coding effort, but will not be pursued here.

# Index

auto-creation 36
base class 29
child window 32
**delete** (keyword) 37
derived class 29
drop-down menu 10
event handler 5
inheritance 29
inheritance of classes 5
instance of a class 4
main window 32

MDI application 34
menu editor 18
menu item 19
multiple document interface (MDI) 34
**new** (keyword) 36
owner of visual object 36
pointer 29
separator 19
shortcut to a menu item 19
**this** (keyword) 36
wrapping 5, 29